CODE
EXTRA

T. rex Trouble

Ian MacDonald • Jonatronix

Forbidden
Valley

OXFORD

UNIVERSITY PRESS

CODE Control Update:

My name is **CODE**. I am the computer that controls **Micro World**. **Team X** and **Mini** are trying to get the **CODE keys** and rescue **Macro Marvel**. My **BITEs** must stop them!

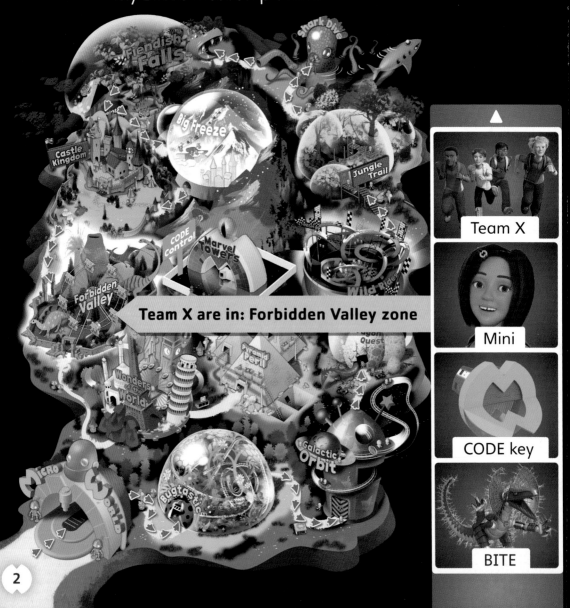

Team X are in: Forbidden Valley zone

Team X

Mini

CODE key

BITE

Forbidden Valley cameras

CAMERA 1 · REC

Cat and Tiger were
trapped on the big wheel.

CAMERA 2 · REC

They escaped using the jet
pack and Bee-machine.

CAMERA 3 · REC

Max, Tiger and Mini fell
into a crack in the ground.

CAMERA 4 · REC

Tiger used the Driller to
get them out.

Status: Max, Tiger and Mini have
split up to look for the BITE.

Before you read

Sound checker

The sound to remember when you are reading this book.

oor   ore   our   oar
ough   augh   al

Word alert

Blend the sounds. Remember the sound you have practised.

p**oor**   t**ore**   f**our**   s**oar**ed
br**ough**t   c**augh**t   w**al**ked

Into the zone

What would you do if you came face to face with a Tyrannosaurus rex?

Chapter 1 – A Mini Rescue

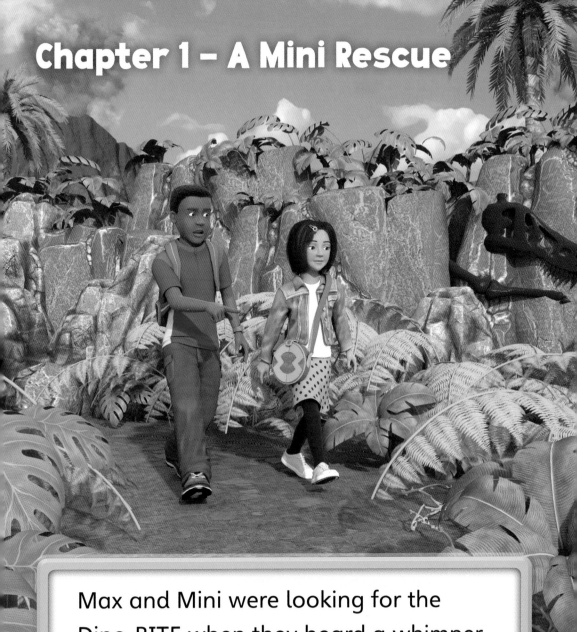

Max and Mini were looking for the Dino-BITE when they heard a whimper. "It came from here," said Max, pointing at a bush.

Max searched among the bushes.
Suddenly, he leapt back.
"It's a baby tyrannosaur!" he cried.

"Poor thing ... its paw is caught on a thorny stalk!" said Mini.
Gently, she untangled the creature.

Max and Mini walked away, but the baby trotted after them.
"Where's your family?" Mini asked the dinosaur. "You need to find them."

Shoo! Naughty dinosaur.

8

Just then, the jungle floor began to tremble.

"It's an earthquake!" exclaimed Mini.

"I don't think so," said Max, but his words were muffled by a mighty roar.

ROAR!

Above them, a huge, scaly head burst through the trees.

"It's Mummy-saurus!" cried Max.
"She thinks we are taking her baby."

Chapter 2 – A Monster Mistake

The friends sped through the jungle as fast as they could travel.

ROAR!

The earth shook as the dinosaur tore after them.

Suddenly, they came to a halt. In front of them was a deep gully.
"What should we do now?" Mini said, with a gulp.

Max thought quickly and pressed his watch. The climbing wire shot out, hooking on to a tree on the other side of the gully. "Hold on!" he yelled.

ROAR! Mini looked back. The tyrannosaur was just four steps away.

"Luckily, I'm less scared of heights than dinosaurs!" said Mini.
She grabbed Max's arm and they jumped.

Chapter 3 – Look Out!

ROAR!

Max and Mini soared across
the whole gully on Max's wire.

They slammed into the rocky wall on the far side. Max pressed his watch but it just whirred like a broken engine.

"Oh no!" he groaned. "The wire is caught!"

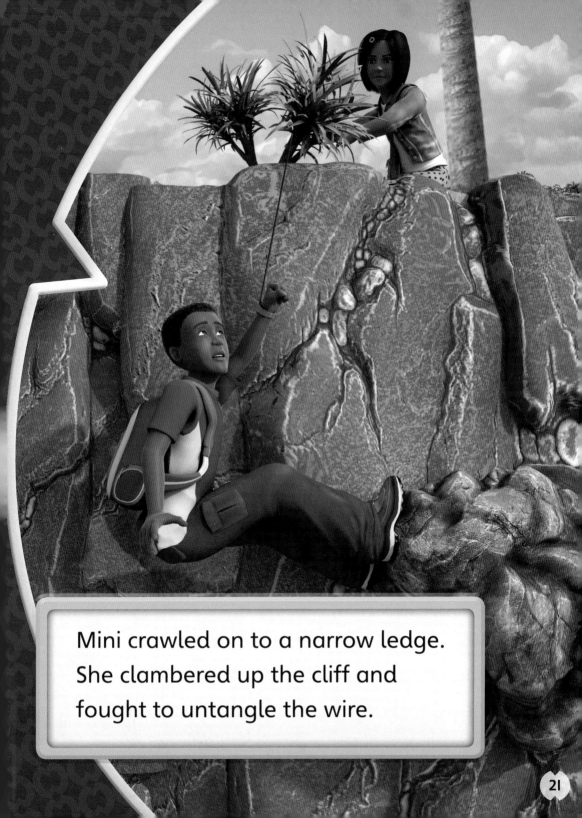

Mini crawled on to a narrow ledge. She clambered up the cliff and fought to untangle the wire.

Max pressed his watch once more and the wire brought him up. They stood looking back at the dinosaurs.